D1739660

SCHOLASTIC

Multimodal Texts

Digital Texts for on-screen literacy lessons

TERMS AND CONDITIONS

IMPORTANT – PERMITTED USE AND WARNINGS – READ CAREFULLY BEFORE USING

Licence

Copyright in the software contained in this CD-ROM and in its accompanying material belongs to Scholastic Limited. All rights reserved. © 2008 Scholastic Ltd.

Save for these purposes, or as expressly authorised in the accompanying materials, the software may not be copied, reproduced, used, sold, licensed, transferred, exchanged, hired, or exported in whole or in part or in any manner or form without the prior written consent of Scholastic Ltd. Any such unauthorised use or activities are prohibited and may give rise to civil liabilities and criminal prosecutions.

The material contained on this CD-ROM may only be used in the context for which it was intended in *Multimodal Texts*, and is for use only in the school which has purchased the book and CD-ROM, or by the teacher who has purchased the book and CD-ROM. Permission to download images is given for purchasers only and not for users from any lending service. Any further use of the material contravenes Scholastic Ltd's copyright and that of other rights holders.

This CD-ROM has been tested for viruses at all stages of its production. However, we recommend that you run virus-checking software on your computer systems at all times. Scholastic Ltd cannot accept any responsibility for any loss, disruption or damage to your data or your computer system that may occur as a result of using either the CD-ROM or the data held on it.

For all technical support queries, please phone Scholastic Customer Services on 0845 603 9091.

Year 6

Scottish Primary Y7

CREDITS

Author
Gill Matthews

Development Editor
Rachel Mackinnon

Editor
Sara Wiegand

Assistant Editor
Kathleen McCully

Series Designers
Micky Pledge and Melissa Leeke

Designer
Micky Pledge

CD-ROM development

CD-ROM developed in association with Infuze Ltd

Acknowledgements

The publishers gratefully acknowledge permission to reproduce the following copyright material:

Favourite Sports, *Victorian Transport: Horses* and *Schiehallion* websites by Sarah Fleming © 2008, Sarah Fleming (2008, previously unpublished). *Solar Crystals* by Adam Guillain © 2008, Adam Guillain (2008, previously unpublished). *Blown up by a bomb* by Fiona Undrill © 2008, Fiona Undrill (2008, previously unpublished). *Sunflowers* by Clare Robertson © 2008, Clare Robertson (2008, previously unpublished). *Vandals!* by Sue Graves © 2008, Sue Graves (2008, previously unpublished). *Salmon Says* by Celia Warren © 2008, Celia Warren (2008, previously unpublished). Extracts from Primary National Strategy's *Primary Framework for Literacy* (2006) www.standards.dfes.gov.uk/primaryframework © Crown copyright. Reproduced under the terms of the Click Use Licence.

Every effort has been made to trace copyright holders for the works reproduced in this book, and the publishers apologise for any inadvertent omissions.

Published by Scholastic Ltd
Villiers House
Clarendon Avenue
Leamington Spa
Warwickshire CV32 5PR
www.scholastic.co.uk

Designed using Adobe InDesign.

Printed in China through Golden Cup Printing Services

1 2 3 4 5 6 7 8 9   8 9 0 1 2 3 4 5 6 7

Text © 2008 Gill Matthews
© 2008 Scholastic Ltd

British Library Cataloguing-in-Publication Data
A catalogue record for this book is available from the British Library.
ISBN 978-1407-10017-3

The right of Gill Matthews to be identified as the author of this work has been asserted by her in accordance with the Copyright, Designs and Patents Act 1988.

All rights reserved. This book is sold subject to the condition that it shall not, by way of trade or otherwise, be lent, hired out or otherwise circulated without the publisher's prior consent in any form of binding or cover other than that in which it is published and without a similar condition, including this condition, being imposed upon the subsequent purchaser.

No part of this publication may be reproduced, stored in a retrieval system, or transmitted, in any form or by any means, electronic, mechanical, photocopying, recording or otherwise, other than for the purposes described in the lessons in this book, without the prior permission of the publisher. This book remains copyright, although permission is granted to copy pages where indicated for classroom distribution and use only in the school which has purchased the book, or by the teacher who has purchased the book, and in accordance with the CLA licensing agreement. Photocopying permission is given only for purchasers and not for borrowers of books from any lending service.

Due to the nature of the web, the publisher cannot guarantee the content or links of any of the websites referred to in this book. It is the responsibility of the reader to assess the suitability of websites. Ensure you read and abide by the terms and conditions of websites when you use material from website links.

Minimum system requirement:
- PC or Mac with a 4x speed CD-ROM drive and 512MB RAM
- Windows 98/2000/XP or Mac OSX 10.2 or later
- Recommended minimum processor speed 900Mhz
- 16bit sound and graphics card

SCHOLASTIC
www.scholastic.co.uk

Contents

Introduction

What are multimodal and digital texts?

Multimodal texts include at least two of the following:
- written text
- images
- sound
- movement or gesture

Digital texts are those which are electronic.

A digital text does not have to be multimodal and a multimodal text does not have to be digital.

Why teach them?

Multimodal texts are all around us, from picture books to information leaflets, and children are exposed to a large amount of digital information through the internet, computer games, television and so on. The DfES document *Multimodal – ICT – Digital texts* says *The texts children read on screen influence their writing.* These texts and their features need to be studied alongside traditional texts. The Revised Literacy Framework recommends that multimodal or digital elements are incorporated into literacy teaching through the use of digital cameras, sound recording software, presentational software and so on. *Multimodal Texts* allows you and your children to explore these text types in a safe environment.

About the product

The CD-ROM provides:
- Three mini-websites – completely self-contained with live links including photographs, video or audio.
- Video – a short film with narration.
- Animation – moving illustration with voice-over.
- Three stories – one with an alternative ending (decide as a class what the characters chose to do), all fully illustrated with audio versions.
- Playscript – with full audio version to listen to and with individual sound effects to use in whole-class re-enactment.
- Poetry – fully illustrated with audio version.
- Podcast and audio – both with a transcript which scrolls as you listen and a PDF version to print.

- Two sequences of images – listen to the related sound effects by clicking on the buttons.
- Photocopiable pages (also provided in the book).

The book contains detailed teaching ideas based on the CD-ROM texts.

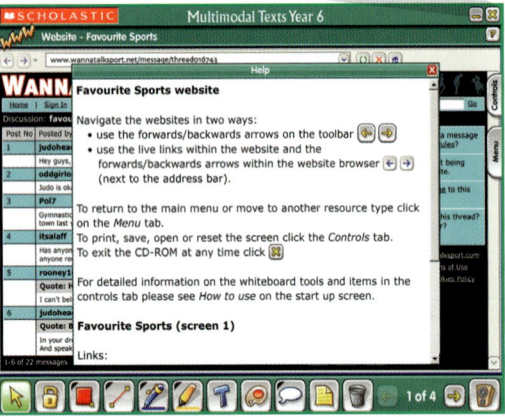

About the CD-ROM

The CD-ROM is installable; follow the text file instructions on the disk to install it on to your system. Once installed, navigate to the program location to open it.

Help

Below are brief guidance notes for using the CD-ROM. For more detailed information see *How to use* on the start-up screen, or see '?' for screen-by-screen help (top right-hand corner of the screen).

Main menu

This screen provides links to all the text types and the photocopiable pages. Click on a text type button to be taken either to the sub-menu or directly to that resource.

SCHOLASTIC
www.scholastic.co.uk

Menu

The menu tab on the right-hand side of the screen allows you to navigate to other areas on the CD-ROM. Click on the tab to open the menu.

Menu

Main Menu
Websites
Video
Animation
Stories
Playscript
Poetry
Podcast
Audio
Images

Printing

All of the resources are printable. For websites, stories, playscripts, poetry and images there are two print options. You can either print the current screen, including annotations (unless annotations are hidden) or you can print a clean set of the entire resource (every screen). For all other resources the current screen will print with any annotations.

Print current screen

Print all screens in current activity

Cancel

Controls

Click on the controls tab on the right-hand side of the screen to access the Print, Open, Save and Reset-screen buttons.

Print (see Printing for more information).

Save all annotations you have made to the texts.

Controls

Open – navigate to your saved file to open your annotations.

Reset the page.

Whiteboard tools

The CD-ROM comes with its own set of whiteboard tools for use on any whiteboard. These include:

Pen tool – draw freehand in three different thicknesses.

Shape tool – add a filled or unfilled circle or square.

Speech/thought bubbles – add a speech or thought bubble.

Text tool – add text using the keyboard.

Rubbish bin – select an annotation and click this button to delete it.

Select tool.

1 of 4

Annotations – on and locked/ hidden and locked/unlocked.

Line tool – draw straight lines in three different thicknesses.

Highlighter tool – highlight in three different thicknesses.

Colour palette – select a colour to annotate in.

Notes – add a sticky-note style box to type in.

Forwards/backwards – navigate between the text pages.

Volume – adjust the volume using the slider, or mute by clicking the speaker icon.

Please note – to access buttons on screen, such as playback buttons, the padlock needs to be in the locked position.

SCHOLASTIC
www.scholastic.co.uk

Favourite Sports

Objectives

- Strand 7: Explore how word meanings change when used in different contexts.
- Strand 9: Use different narrative techniques to engage and entertain the reader.

Differentiation

Support
- The children can look up the word 'icon' in an etymological dictionary and decide which definition is relevant to the meaning of the word emoticon.

Extend
- The children can create a dictionary of emoticons using the typical layout and format of a dictionary (for example, emoticon followed by the definition).

Cross-curricular activities

ICT Unit 4A Writing for different audiences
- Develop a class blog about a specific subject (for example, hobbies or pets).

Whiteboard tools

- Whiteboard tools used on the screen shots include:
- Outline circle
- Text tool
- Colours used

How the text works and responding to the text

- Discuss the children's experience of websites. Ask: *When do you use them? Why do you use them?* Invite the children, in pairs, to discuss what they know about websites. They should focus particularly on the organisational and navigational features.

- Take feedback from the discussion and list the children's responses. Explore the similarities and differences between websites and books. Hand out photocopiable page 34 'Venn diagram' for the children to complete. Which would the children prefer to use to find information (websites or books)?

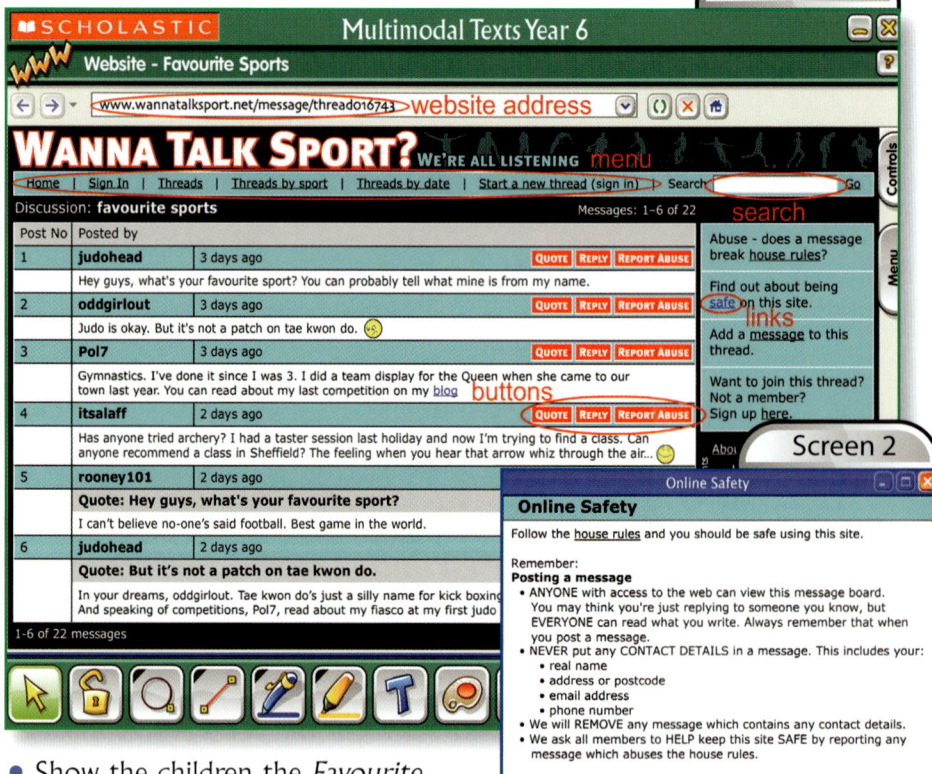

- Show the children the *Favourite Sports* home page. Identify some of the organisational and navigational features listed earlier. Ask: *Are you able to add any further features to the list from this page?*

- Establish that this particular website is a message board for discussing different sports. Ask the children to identify the ways in which the messages can be accessed (for example, by date or by sport).

- Focus the children's attention on the menu on the right-hand side of the screen. Discuss why a user of the site might need to know about being safe. Click on the link *safe*, and ensure that the children understand why the advice is being given.

- Return to the message board and identify how the messages are organised (in the order they were posted, shown by the number of days). Read message one and ask the children to respond to the question. Take feedback, encouraging the children to express whether they have a favourite sport. List the sports that the children mention. Display the complete message board. Ask: *Is your favourite sport mentioned?*

SCHOLASTIC
www.scholastic.co.uk

- Focus on the three smiley faces. Do the children know what this type of image is called? (Emoticon.) Why might the message posters have added them? (To show how they are feeling.) Ask: *Do you know any other emoticons?* Explain that when computer users first started using emoticons, they used punctuation marks to create them, and that more recent software turns the punctuation marks into pictures, like the smiley faces. You may wish to demonstrate this by typing a colon and a bracket :). Explain that the word emoticon is a 'portmanteau' – a word blending the sounds and combining the meanings of two other words. In this case, the words are 'emotion' and 'icon'.

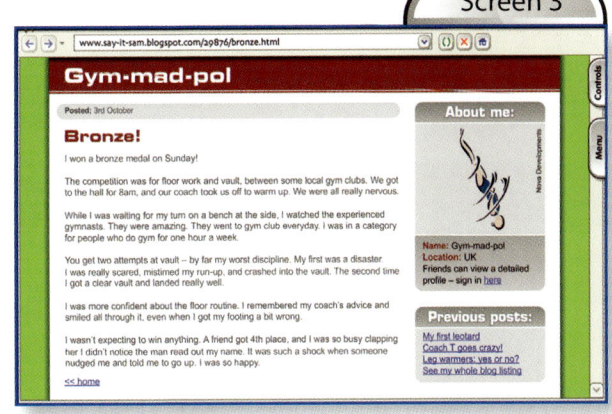

- Read message three and ask the children what their understanding of a blog is. Explain that this is also formed from two words (web and log). Click on the link to Pol7's blog. Read the entry and discuss its style and tone with the children (fairly chatty and informal).

- Ask the children to identify some of the technical vocabulary that is connected with gymnastics (for example, *vault*, *discipline* and *floor routine*) and to work out what the words mean.

- Return to the message board and read message six. Ask the children what they think the word *fiasco* means. Challenge them, in pairs, to come up with alternative words that have a similar meaning.

- Click on the link to judohead's blog. Ask the children to read it and discuss whether or not they feel that judohead's first judo competition really was a fiasco. Compare the style and tone with Pol7's entry. Is it also informal?

Writing activities

- Explain to the children that they are going to write a response to judohead's message. Ask them, in pairs, to discuss what they might say in their reply. They can orally rehearse their replies, focusing particularly on the style and tone, before writing their responses.

- Ask the children to write a blog about their favourite sport. Encourage them to explore why they like the sport, whether they take part in it and/or watch it.

Assessment

- As a class, review the blog entries. Do the children find the subject matter interesting and entertaining? Are the blog entries written in an appropriate style? Encourage the children to make constructive comments as to how entries could be improved.

Reference to *100 Literacy Framework Lessons*

- Non-fiction Unit 4 Formal/impersonal writing pages 119–134

Photocopiable

- See page 34 or CD-ROM.

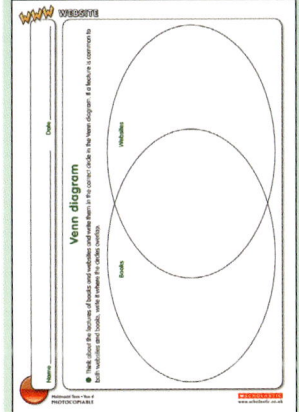

SCHOLASTIC
www.scholastic.co.uk

Victorian Transport: Horses

Objective

● Strand 7: Appraise a text quickly, deciding on its value, quality or usefulness.

Differentiation

Support

● Help the children to develop the skills needed to make inferences and deductions from visual images. Draw their attention to specific parts of images and prompt responses by asking questions that start with *Why do you think...?* and *How would you have felt...?*

Extend

● Ask the children to look at the design of the website and in particular the combination of texts and images, the use of colour, layout, fonts and typefaces. They can then write a constructive critique to be presented to the website designers, highlighting the positive aspects and making suggestions for improvements.

Cross-curricular activities

History Unit 18
What was it like to be here in the past?
● The children can research other aspects of transport in Victorian times and write it as another page to be added to the website.

How the text works

● Show the children screen 1 of the website *Victorian Transport: Horses.* Ask: *Who do you think might access this website? What could they be looking for?* Check that the children can identify the address of the website.

● Ask the children how they would get an overview of the content of a website. Click on the site map link (in the small print at the bottom of the screen, this will take you to screen 5). Ask the children to identify how the site is organised (by form of transport). Click on the *London* link under the *Horses* heading to return to screen 1.

● Together, look at the photographs, encouraging the children to make inferences and deductions about life in Victorian times (for example, there were no cars).

● Read the first paragraph on this screen, referring to the table of new forms of transport for extra information. Ask: *Are you surprised by anything you have read so far?* Check the children's understanding of the different forms of transport.

SCHOLASTIC
www.scholastic.co.uk

- Read paragraphs two and three on screen 1. Ask the children to identify the link that takes the user to more information about recycling horse manure (*here* in the green box on the left-hand side of the screen). Can they suggest how the manure might have been recycled? Click on the link.

- Focus the children's attention on the map on screen 4. Ask the children to read the map and to tell you the information they can glean from it. Support their reading by asking: *How was the manure transported out of London?* (By barge.) *What came back into London on the barges?* (Food.) Can the children suggest why food had to be brought into London? (Crops were grown in rural areas, not in cities.) Read the text about manure recycling on this page to confirm the children's responses.

- Return to the home page and read the final paragraph. Explain that Anna Sewell wrote *Black Beauty* to draw people's attention to the suffering and cruel treatment of working horses at the time. Click on the audio link and listen to the extract. Ask: *What do you think life must have been like for horses that pulled cabs?*

Responding to the text

- Hand out photocopiable page 35 'Understanding the text' and ask the children to complete it independently, or in pairs, to check their comprehension.

- Involve the children in reflecting on what they have learned about horse-drawn transport in Victorian times and about how they used the website. Discuss with the children whether they prefer to use paper-based or on-line texts, encouraging them to support their opinions with sound reasons.

Writing activities

- Discuss with the children any new or unfamiliar words that they have come across on the website. Invite them to read some dictionary definitions and discuss how definitions are worded. Explain to the children that they are going to write definitions for some of the words on the website. Ask the children, in pairs, to identify one word, to talk about what they think it means and then to create a definition. Share these with the rest of the class, correcting any misconceptions or misunderstandings about the word meanings.

Assessment

- Ask the children to present some of the written information on the website into a visual image (for example, a chart, table or diagram). They can explain how and why it is easier to read as a visual text.

Reference to *100 Literacy Framework Lessons*

- Non-fiction Unit 4 Formal/impersonal writing pages 126–127

Photocopiable

- See page 35 or CD-ROM.

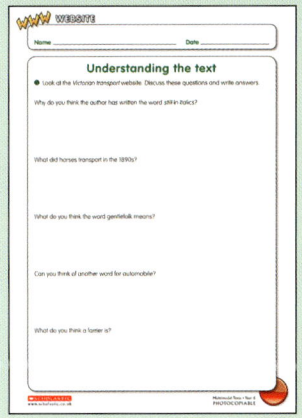

Screen 5

Schiehallion

Objectives

● Strand 2: Make notes when listening for a sustained period and discuss how note-taking varies depending on context and purpose.
● Strand 7: Understand underlying themes, causes and points of view.

Differentiation

Support
● Work with the children as they make notes, helping them to identify important sentences, the main point of a sentence and key words.

Extend
● Remind the children that when they make notes they are for their own reference; it doesn't matter too much if someone else can't read them all, or doesn't understand them. Discuss how they can develop their own abbreviations for words to speed up the note-making process (for example, by leaving out the vowels).

Cross-curricular activities

ICT Unit 6A
Multimedia presentation
● The children can design and produce a web page that incorporates text, images and hyperlinks to sound effects or video.

Whiteboard tools

● Whiteboard tools used on the screen shots include:
Q Outline circle
✎ Line tool
🖊 Highlighter
T Text tool
◉ Colours used ● ●

How the text works and responding to the text

● Show the children screen 1 of the website. Ask: *What sort of text is it?* (A blog.) Discuss their experience of blogs and blogging, exploring why people post blogs, and who might read them.

● Read the first section of the blog (up to the *pros and cons* box). Ask: *Who might be interested in reading this?* (Other walkers.) Draw the children's attention to the fairly informal style.

● Discuss how the children think the blogger felt about 'bagging their first Munro'. Refer the children to the blogger's name (*Hard as Nails*). Ask: *What does this tell you about him/her? What gender do you think the blogger is?*

● Explore the children's understanding of some of the more challenging technical vocabulary (for example, *gruelling*, *restored* and *erode*).

● Draw the children's attention to the two links at the bottom of the screen 1 and explain that you are going to look for more information about paths on mountains. Click on the first link.

● Focus the children's attention on the map and ask whether they have seen or used similar maps. Explain that maps such as this one show the contours and height of the landscape and that the closer the contour lines are together, the steeper the terrain. Ask the children to identify the old path and the new path.

● Read the heading at the top of the page, *Is it right to make hill walkers keep to a paved path?* Read the subheading, drawing the children's attention to the word *discussion*. Ask: *What do you understand by this word? What would you expect to find in a discussion text?* (Points for and against an issue.)

● Read the rest of the text. Encourage the children to note down the

SCHOLASTIC
www.scholastic.co.uk

points for and against making hill walkers use a paved path, using photocopiable page 36 'For and against'. Ask: *Do you think that this is a balanced discussion, or does the author show a bias towards a particular view?*

- Discuss the note-making activity and any techniques the children used that they found helpful (for example, noting key words and phrases).

- Return to the blogger's list of *pros and cons* on screen 1 and compare these with the points that the children have noted. Discuss any similarities and differences.

- Compare the informality of the blog with the more formal style and tone of the text on screen 2.

- Return to screen 1 and click on the link for information about Schiehallion. Ask the children to look carefully at the photograph. What information can they glean about the mountain from it?

- Draw the children's attention to the way the text on this page is organised. (Grouped under headings.) Discuss why it might be organised in this way. Does it make it easier to read?

- Read through the text, checking the children's understanding of new or unfamiliar vocabulary (for example, *heathland*, *summit*, *occupation* and *cairn*).

Writing activities

- To prepare the children for writing, hold a whole-class discussion on an issue that is relevant to the children, in the school or the local area. During the discussion, focus on the development of different points of view. As a class, list the pros and cons of the issue that you have just explored.

- Explore the children's knowledge and understanding of the structure of a discussion text. (For example: introduce the issue; put forward one point of view; put forward an alternative point of view; summarise the discussion.) Ask the children, in small groups, to discuss another relevant issue. They then list the pros and cons of the issue and write a complete discussion text.

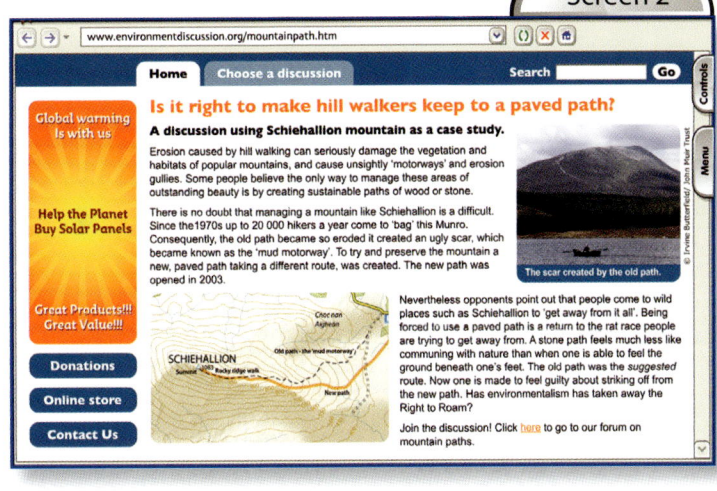

Screen 2

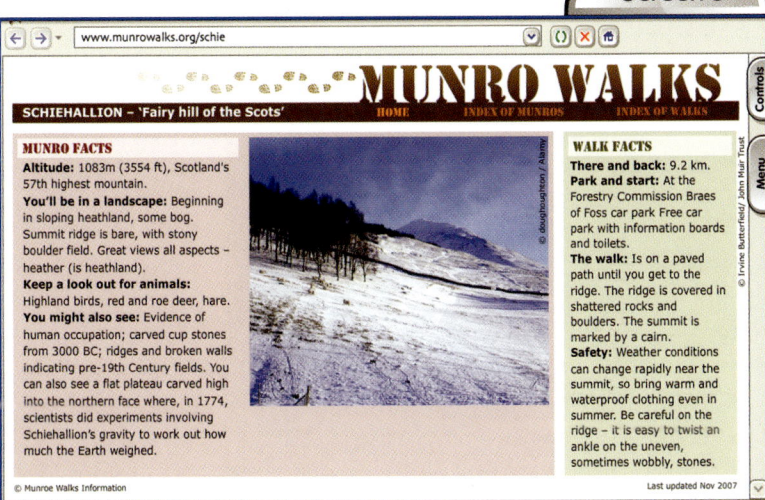

Screen 3

Assessment

- As the children are exploring points of view in the text and looking for evidence of balance and bias, ask questions that explore their understanding of this, for example: *What does the author really feel about this issue? How do you know?*

Reference to *100 Literacy Framework Lessons*

- Non-fiction Unit 3 Argument pages 103–118

Photocopiable

- See page 36 or CD-ROM.

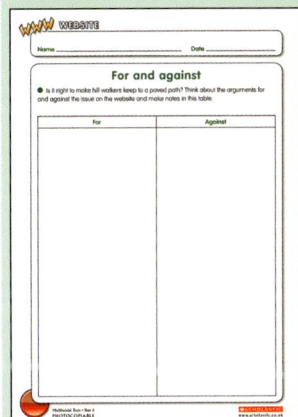

Objectives

- Strand 1: Participate in whole-class debate using the conventions and language of debate, including Standard English.
- Strand 2: Make notes when listening for a sustained period and discuss how note-taking varies depending on context and purpose.

Differentiation

Support
- Support the children by offering the writing frame on photocopiable page 37 'Planning a discussion text' when they are in the planning stages.

Extend
- Ask the children to structure their discussion text in a slightly different way; rather than having a paragraph for the issue and a paragraph against, the children can present an argument for the issue, and then follow it with a counter argument. This argument/counter argument structure can continue throughout the text.

Cross-curricular activities

Geography Unit 6
Investigating our local area
- The children can research areas where housing and other buildings have been built on flood plains, and they can explore the impact of such developments.

Building on the flood plain

How the text works and responding to the text

- Explain to the children that they are going to watch a news clip with the sound turned off. (To mute the video click on the speaker image on the toolbar and then click the speaker icon so it has a cross through it.) The main focus is to identify what they think the clip is about. Emphasise that as it is from a news programme, the clip will be about something newsworthy.

- Show the children the clip and give them a few minutes to discuss it with a partner. Take feedback, asking the children to support their responses with evidence from the clip or from their own experience.

- Ask the children what they think the reporter might be saying during the film. Invite them, in pairs, to orally rehearse the voice-over for the news clip and then to make notes.

- Ask some of the children to present their voice-overs to the rest of the class. Discuss the similarities and differences between the content of the voice-overs.

- Play the news clip with the sound, encouraging the children to listen carefully to the voice-over. Ask: *Were you accurate in your interpretations of what*

SCHOLASTIC
www.scholastic.co.uk

the news clip was about? Discuss the focus of the news clip. (The issue of building houses on the flood plain.)

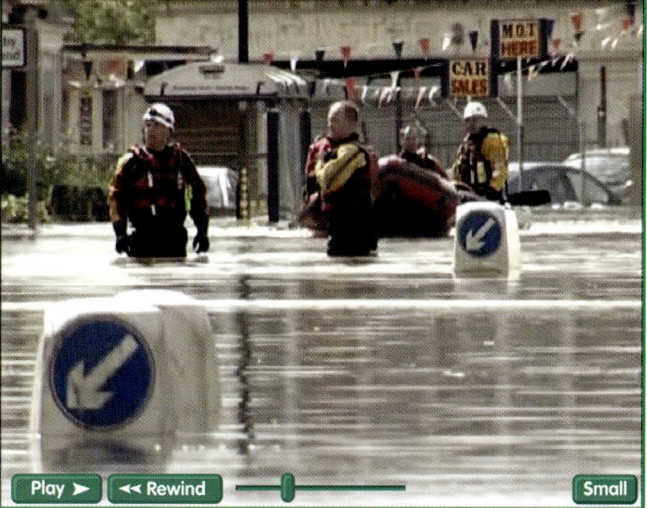

- Ask the children some literal questions about the content of the voice-over, for example: *What is the only way to move around? What have the fire service been doing?*

- Play the news clip again, ask the children to think about why the houses might be flooded. (They were built on a flood plain.) Discuss with the children why houses might have been built in these areas. Ask them to think about points for and against it.

- Introduce the idea of holding a formal debate and explain how they operate. For example: a chair person is appointed to manage the debate; a proposal is put forward; debaters take turns to offer reasons and evidence for or against the proposal; the chair person decides on the conclusions reached, based on the views heard.

- Involve the class in nominating a chair and main speakers. You may wish other children to take on the roles of interested or involved parties (for example, local residents, shopkeepers or local councillors).

- On the whiteboard, write the title of the debate, 'Should houses be built on flood plains?' Carry out the debate, and finish by asking the chair to summarise what they heard. Ask: *Can you draw any conclusions from the debate or does the issue remain unresolved?*

Writing activities

- Explain to the children that they are going to use the content of the debate, to write to the local council, offering a balanced view of the issue. Discuss the degree of formality that would be needed. Ask the children, in small groups, to discuss and note down the main points, and to orally rehearse how they might put these across. Are they formal enough, or too formal in style? The children can write up the content of the debate as a discussion text, using the typical structural and linguistic features of the text type.

Assessment

- Are the children aware of the purpose of discussion texts?
- Are they able to produce a discussion text that follows a coherent structure and uses some typical language features? (For example, logical connectives and some use of the passive voice.)

Reference to *100 Literacy Framework Lessons*

- Non-fiction Unit 3 Argument pages 103–118

Photocopiable

- See page 37 or CD-ROM.

Video © ITN Source

Headland erosion

Objectives

● Strand 2: Make notes when listening for a sustained period and discuss how note-taking varies depending on context and purpose.
● Strand 7: Understand how writers use different structures to create coherence and impact.

Differentiation

Support
● Work with the children during the note-making session, supporting them in identifying key information and noting down key words, rather than trying to write down all of the spoken text. Encourage them to make links between what they are hearing, and the images that they are seeing.
Extend
● Remind the children of work they have done previously on explanations. Create a word bank of cause and effect connectives and encourage the children to include these in their written explanations.

Cross-curricular activities

Geography Unit 7
Weather around the world
● Explore and explain other situations where erosion occurs.

How the text works

● Explain to the children that they are going to watch a brief animation. Play the animation without the sound (adjust the sound using the speaker on the toolbar), asking the children to focus on what is happening.

● Ask them, in pairs, to discuss what they saw and what they think was happening. Take feedback from the discussion. Ask the children to think about any technical (geographical) vocabulary that they used during their discussions.

● Play the animation again, this time with the sound. Ask: *What sort of text are you seeing and hearing on the animation?* (Non-fiction.) *What is the purpose of the text?* (To explain a process.) Ask the children to talk about explanations. Ask them when they read/see explanations and when they speak or write explanations.

Responding to the text

● Replay the animation, asking the children to note down any technical vocabulary that they hear (for example, *erodes*, *headland*, *stack*). Take feedback and list the vocabulary that the children identified. Work

SCHOLASTIC
www.scholastic.co.uk

through the list and check the children's understanding of the words. Replay the animation to see if they can work out any unfamiliar vocabulary from the information shown.

- Explore why the children think the author of this text chose to use an animation rather than just a written explanation. Ask: *Do you find it is easier to understand when you can see the animation?*

- Give the children the opportunity to view the animation a number of times. Ask them to focus on the stages in the erosion process, making notes as they watch and listen to the animation. Ask: *How many stages are there in the erosion process?* (Five.)

- Discuss how the children tackled the note-making process. Did they note down key words, number the stages or make sketches?

- Ask them to tell a partner about the erosion process, using their notes as prompts. Did they find that their notes helped them or did they find that they had not recorded enough information?

- Replay the animation, asking the children to focus on the structure and organisation of the text. Ask: *Is the chronological order important?* (Yes, it wouldn't make sense otherwise.)

- Encourage the children to listen for words in the voice-over that are related to time (for example, *until*, *eventually*, *finally*). Build up a class list of time connectives that they can refer to when writing chronologically ordered texts themselves. Encourage the children to add to this list if they find other time connectives in their reading.

- Discuss the tense of the explanation (present).

Writing activities

- Explain to the children that they are going to amend the information given in the animation to be presented to younger children. Remind them to use the time connective list developed earlier. Encourage them to present their explanation using ICT (for example, photographs, diagrams or a flowchart using presentation software). Discuss the impact of adding sound effects or music to the presentation. If possible, arrange for them to make their presentation to a younger year group.

- Revisit the animation and ask the children to think about presenting the information as a poem. Ask them to concentrate on the sounds of the waves and to develop a list of adjectives that describe what they can hear. Encourage the children to imagine that they are standing on the cliff top and to think about what they could smell, taste and feel, noting down their ideas on photocopiable page 38 'Descriptive thinking'. In pairs, ask the children to develop their own erosion poems. Carry out a 'poetry slam' in which the children present their poems to the rest of the class.

Animation © Andy Keylock/Beehive Illustration

Assessment

- Are the children using the typical structural (introduction, sequenced explanation) and linguistic (present tense, time connectives, cause and effect connectives, technical vocabulary) forms of explanation?

Reference to *100 Literacy Framework Lessons*

- Poetry Unit 1 The power of imagery pages 135–148

Photocopiable

- See page 38 or CD-ROM.

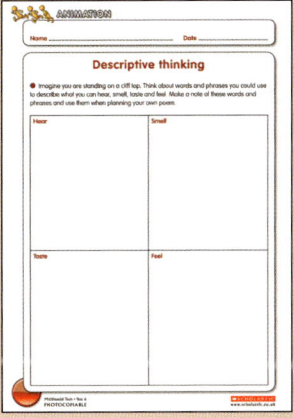

Solar Crystals

Objectives

● Strand 4: Improvise using a range of drama strategies and conventions to explore themes such as hopes, fears and desires.
● Strand 7: Understand underlying themes, causes and points of view.

Differentiation

Support
● Work with the children in identifying problems that humans might have created on other planets, and how these could be put right. Discuss how they can structure their stories effectively (for example, opening, build up, complication, solution and ending). The children can use photocopiable page 39 'Planning a story' for support in planning.
Extend
● Encourage the children to add dialogue that moves their stories on; from one setting to another and from one action to another.

Cross-curricular activities

Geography Unit 8 Improving the environment
● The children can investigate alternative sustainable energy sources (for example, wind turbines and hydro power).

Whiteboard tools

● Whiteboard tools used on the screen shots include:
🔍 Outline circle
🖊 Pen tool
T Text tool
⬤ Colour used ●

How the text works

● Show the children the title screen of the story *Solar Crystals*. Ask them to think about possible genres that the story might fit into. Take feedback, discussing the evidence they have for suggesting particular genres. Move on to the next illustration. Ask: *Does this confirm your predictions?*

● Discuss the children's knowledge and understanding of the science fiction genre. List any typical features of the genre (for example, often set in outer space, characters may be aliens, and can be set in the future).

● Read or listen to the story up to and including screen 8. Explain that before they choose an ending, they are going to re-read the text, gathering clues and evidence that will influence their choice.

● Return to the title screen. Focus on the title of the story and explore the children's understanding of the word *Solar*. Use an etymological dictionary to investigate the origin of the word.

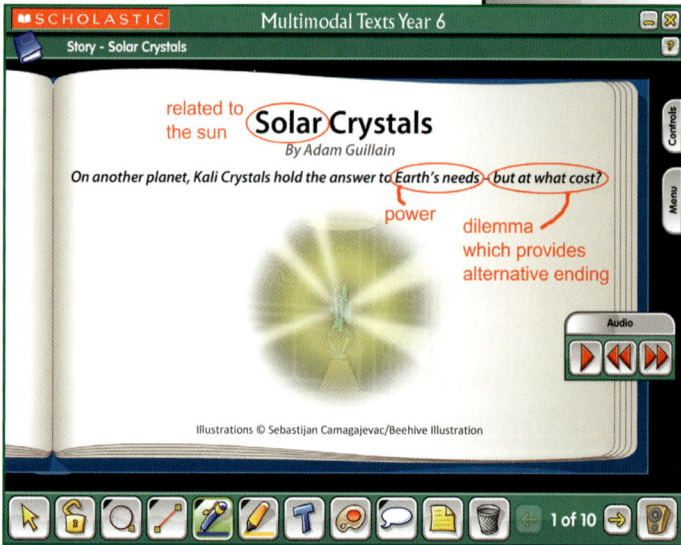

Responding to the text

● Ask the children to read the sentence on the title screen carefully. Having read some of the story, what do they think Earth's needs are? (Power.) What is the meaning of *but at what cost?*

● Go to the next screen and discuss the meaning of the final sentence. Ask: *What does this tell us about the purpose of the Explorer's mission?* (They were searching for something to replace Earth's natural resources.)

● Read through the rest of the story again up to screen 8. As you read, ask questions that encourage the children to make inferences and deductions from the text. For example: *Why was the Admiral excited about the discovery of the new planet? Why did the explorers collect samples of rock and animal life? Why were the Kali crystals 'the answer to all our problems'?*

● Ask: *What would you have done if you were a member of the Explorer's crew?* Carry out a class role play that recreates the argument that took place between the crew and the Admiral about the crystals. Nominate one child to be the Admiral. He/she must make the final decision based on what they have heard. Follow the version of the story decided by the child in role as the Admiral. As a class, discuss whether that was the right thing to do.

SCHOLASTIC
www.scholastic.co.uk

Illustrations © Sebastijan Camagajevac/Beehive Illustration

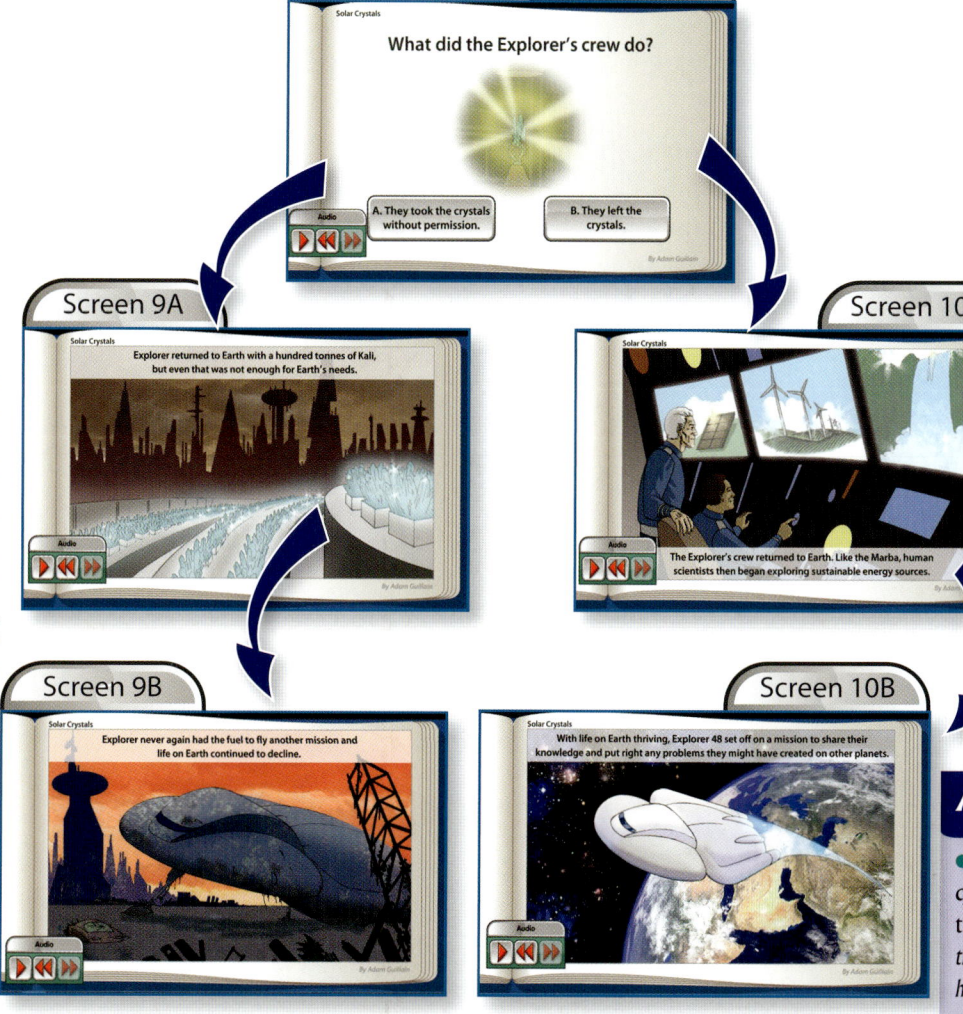

- Invite the children to predict the alternative ending. Follow that version and discuss whether that would have been the right thing to do, and how accurate the children's predictions were.

- Write the headings 'Likes', 'Dislikes', 'Puzzles' and 'Patterns' on the board. Talk through each one, encouraging the children to contribute to each heading based on their response to the story *Solar Crystals*. Focus on the fact that what one child might have liked about the story, another might have disliked. Emphasise that responses to any story will vary from reader to reader.

- Return to the list of typical features of the science fiction genre. Ask: *Which ones have appeared in this story? Can you add any further features to the list?*

Writing activities

- Ask the children to think about the story from the point of view of the Marba people. In groups, invite them to role play particular points in the story when the Marba interact with the crew of the Explorer. Discuss how this helps them to see the story from another point of view. As a class, list the key events in the story. Ask the children to use this list of key events to rewrite the story, as told by one of the Marba.

- Revisit the ending in the story where Explorer 48 is mentioned. In small groups, ask the children to plan the story of Explorer 48's mission and invite some groups to share their ideas with the rest of the class. Children then write their own story of Explorer 48's mission.

Assessment

- Ask the children questions about the story that start with *Why do you think...?* and *How would you have felt...?* Are they able to make inferential responses that draw on their own experiences and refer to evidence within the text?

Reference to *100 Literacy Framework Lessons*

- Narrative Unit 1 Fiction genres pages 9–26

Photocopiable

- See page 39 or CD-ROM.

www.scholastic.co.uk

Blown up by a bomb

Objectives

● Strand 4: Improvise using a range of drama strategies and conventions to explore themes such as hopes, fears and desires.
● Strand 8: Compare how writers from different times and places present experiences and use language.

Differentiation

Support
● Help the children to make inferences from the text by drawing their attention to clues in the text and by asking questions that draw out their knowledge of the Second World War.
Extend
● Ask the children to develop a series of other questions about the story that would mean a reader would have to read between the lines and make inferences and deductions.

Cross-curricular activities

History Unit 9
What was it like for children in the Second World War?
● Ask the children to carry out research in order to find out whether the children in their area were evacuated, or whether local families had evacuees placed with them.

How the text works

● Show the children the illustration on screen 2 without the text or audio (you can hide the text using the shape tool). Ask them to look closely at the detail in the illustration and to identify the setting. Remind them that the setting of a story includes both where and when it is taking place.

● Ask: *When do you think the story is set?* (During the Second World War.) *Where does it take place?* (In a railway station.) Which details in the illustration did they use to help them work out the setting?

● Ask: *What do you think is happening in the illustration?* (Evacuees are being sent out of a city.) Explore their knowledge and understanding of evacuation during the Second World War. Establish that the text they are going to read is in the historical story genre.

Screen 2

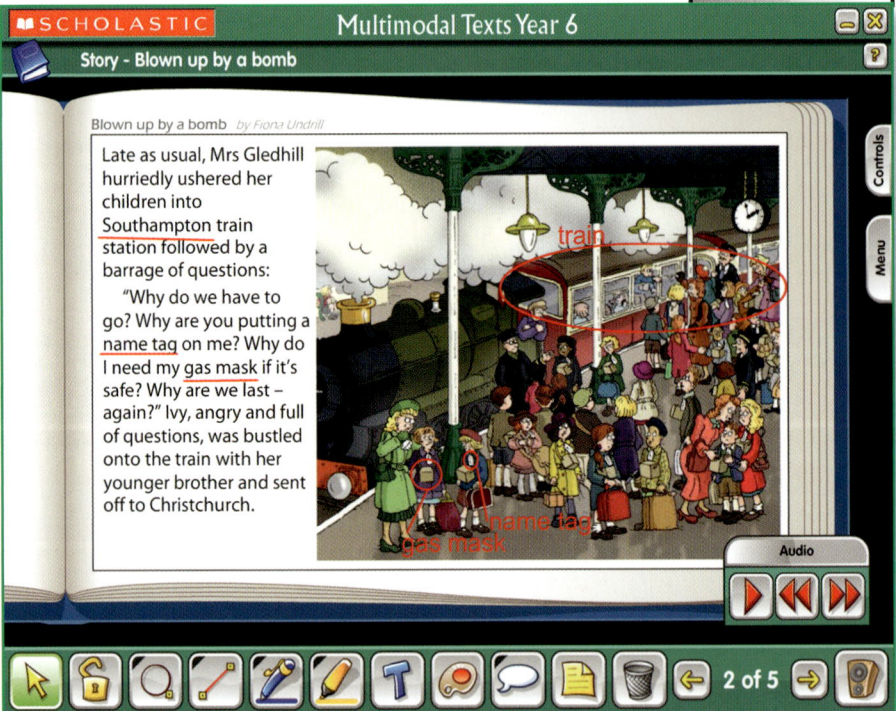

● Show the text on screen 2 and ask the children to identify, and highlight, the evidence that tells the reader about the setting (*Southampton, name tag, gas mask*). Discuss how their knowledge of the Second World War means that they are able to link these words and phrases with the setting.

Screen 3

● Read the rest of the story, pausing after the guard has told Ivy and her brother that the train has been blown up, to ask for predictions as to how the story might end. Read to the end of the story. Ask: *Was your prediction accurate? Do you feel that the ending was a satisfactory one?* Did anyone pick up on the clues about Mrs Gledhill's tendency to be late at the beginning of the story?

■■SCHOLASTIC
www.scholastic.co.uk

Responding to the text

- Return to screen 2 and read the text. Ask: *What sort of atmosphere is created in this opening?* (A sense of urgency.) Identify how the author has created this atmosphere: for example, through careful vocabulary choices (*hurriedly*, *bustled*), or with the string of questions that Ivy asks.

- Read the text on screen 3. Ask the class what they think the word *surrogate* means (substitute). Discuss how they can use the rest of the sentence, with their knowledge of evacuees, to work out the meaning of the word.

- Re-read the rest of the story, asking questions that will evoke deductive and inferential responses. For example: *Why do you think the children had more food on the farm than when they were at home? Why do you think they had to pluck up courage to ask where the train was? How do you think Ivy's mother was feeling when she missed her train?*

- Focus on screen 4, when Ivy and her brother are waiting for the train. Ask: *How did the children find out that the train had been blown up?* (The guard told them.) Discuss whether he had really thought about his answer before telling them. In groups of three, ask the children to explore through role play alternative ways that the guard might have broken the news to Ivy and her brother.

Writing activities

- In groups, ask the children to role play the part of the story when the children arrive in Christchurch and are being told where they will live. Encourage them to use the prompts on photocopiable page 40 'Role play' to support their role play and to make notes in preparation for writing. Discuss how the evacuees must have felt when they were being 'chosen' by their surrogate families. Were these feelings evident in the role play? Model how they can turn their role-play notes into another scene for the story. Once they are happy with their plans, the children can write this scene into the story.

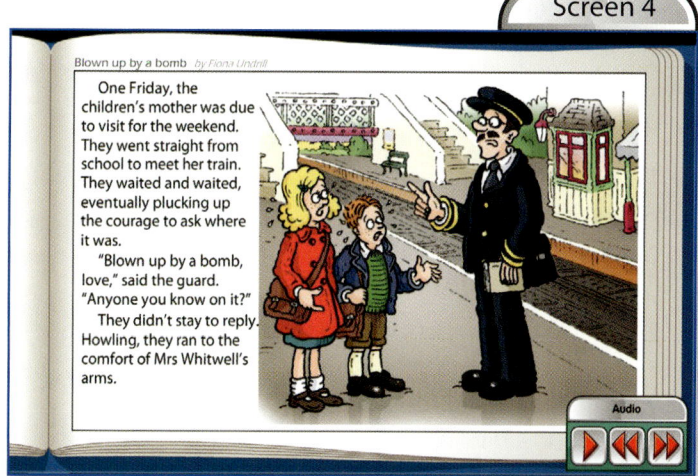

Screen 4

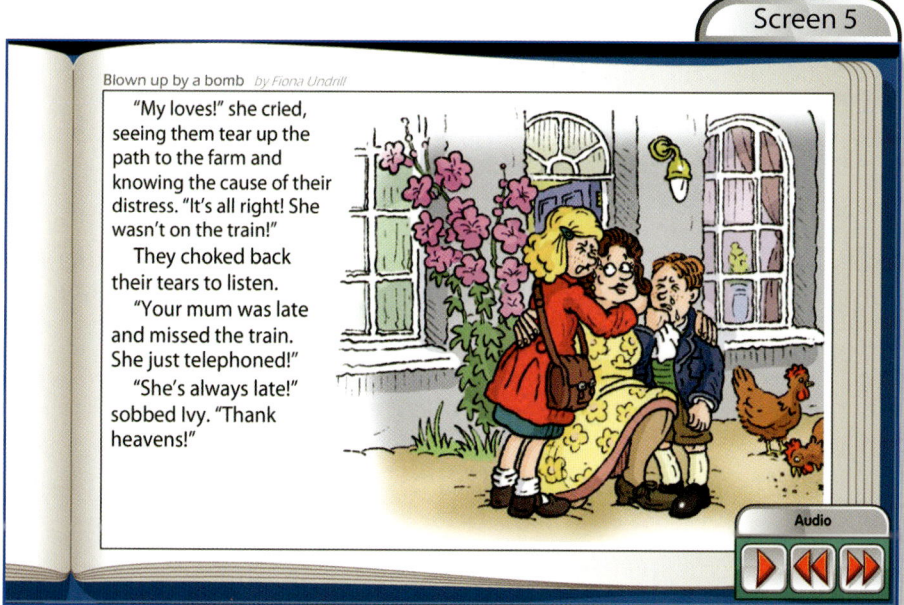

Screen 5

Whiteboard tools

- Whiteboard tools used on the screen shots include:
  - Outline circle
  - Line tool
  - Text tool
  - Colour used ●

Assessment

- Ask the children questions about the story that begin: *Why do you think...?* and *How would you have felt...?* Are they able to make inferential responses that draw on their own experiences and refer to evidence within the text?

Reference to *100 Literacy Framework Lessons*

- Narrative Unit 1 Fiction genres pages 9–26

Photocopiable

- See page 40 or CD-ROM.

Illustrations © Gemma Hastilow/Beehive Illustration

SCHOLASTIC
www.scholastic.co.uk

Sunflowers

Objectives

- Strand 4: Improvise using a range of drama strategies and conventions to explore themes such as hopes, fears and desires.
- Strand 7: Understand underlying themes, causes and points of view.

Differentiation

Support
- Work with the children to plan a simple flashback story in which the main character remembers an earlier event.

Extend
- Support the children in taking and uploading digital images to illustrate their flashback stories.

Cross-curricular activities

PSHE
- Explore situations when the children have felt uncomfortable about their behaviour, discussing how they might have dealt with the situation in other ways.

How the text works

- Read or listen to the story with the children, asking them to think about the underlying theme. Discuss this, focusing on how the children think that Tara is feeling throughout the story (guilty). Ask: *Do you think she feels differently at the end of the story? Why?* Explain that they are going to go back through the story to find clues about Tara's feelings.

- Return to screen 2 and ask the children to find evidence in both the text and the illustrations about how Tara is feeling (for example, her facial expression or *she felt a pain of sadness*).

Screen 2

- Go to screen 3 and ask the children what Tara is doing (remembering an event earlier in the year). Explain that this technique is called a 'flashback'. Ask why the author has said *her stomach ache grew as she remembered that day in the spring.* (She was feeling upset.)

- Continue to screen 4. Ask: *How do you think Tara is feeling?* (Cross.) *Why is she feeling this way?* (She wanted to go shopping rather than working on the allotment.)

- Read screen 5 and ask: *How is Tara feeling?* (Guilty.) *Why?* (She hadn't been very nice to Grandpa Pete.) Where do the children think she is going when she walks away?

- Go to the final screen. Ask: *Where do you think Tara got the sunflowers?* (The allotment.) *What clues are there that the flowers came from the allotment rather than a florist?* (The green gardening twine.) Do the children think that Tara feels less guilty having got Grandpa Pete some of his favourite flowers?

Screen 3

■SCHOLASTIC
www.scholastic.co.uk

Responding to the text

- Focus on screen 5. Ask two of the children to carry out a freeze-frame drama activity that shows through body language how Tara and Grandpa Pete are feeling at this point in the story. Ask the rest of the class to write thought bubbles for the two characters, invite children to write their examples on the whiteboard using the thought-bubble tool.

- Explain to the children that Tara's mum thinks that Tara is upset because Grandpa is in hospital; she doesn't realise that Tara also feels guilty because she didn't treat him very well that day on the allotment. Ask the children in pairs to role play the scene where Tara confesses to her mum why she is upset.

- Take feedback from the role play and discuss how role playing a scenario can help to understand characters' feelings and emotions.

- Return to screen 6 and ask the children to think about what might happen next in the story. Ask for a volunteer to take on the role of Grandpa Pete once he has recovered from his operation. Carry out a hot-seating activity, where the children question Grandpa Pete about how he feels about Tara. Use photocopiable page 41 'Hot-seating questions'.

Writing activities

- Ask the children to write the next scene in the story, using information gained during the various drama activities to add details to their story. Remind the children that the story contained a flashback scene in which Tara remembered an earlier event. Discuss other flashback or time shift techniques; for example, a dream or entering another world via a 'loophole' in time (such as, when Alice falls down the rabbit hole in *Alice in Wonderland*). Ask the children to plan and write their own flashback story.

Screen 4

"Grandpa's here, Tara. He'd like some help on the allotment."
Tara was furious. Mum hadn't even asked her, and now she would have to spend all day on a boring patch of mud.
At the allotment, Grandpa Pete gave Tara some sunflower seeds to plant.
"My favourites" he said. "They always turn to face the sun."

Whiteboard tools

- Whiteboard tools used on the screen shots include:
- Pen tool
- Text tool
- Thought bubble
- Colour used ●

Assessment

- Observe the children as they explore the text through the various drama activities. Are they able to interpret and explore the characters' feelings effectively? Encourage them to reflect on and review their knowledge and understanding.

Reference to *100 Literacy Framework Lessons*

- Narrative Unit 4 short stories with flashbacks pages 55–68

Photocopiable

- See page 41 or CD-ROM.

Screen 5

Tara didn't reply. She shoved the seeds into the ground, and turned her back on him. Later on, he offered her a ham sandwich, and she took it without speaking. She didn't even say thank you.
And now he was lying here, and she couldn't thank him for being kind to her that day – and all the other times. She turned and walked away, tears in her eyes.

Screen 6

Later that afternoon, Tara returned to the ward. Her mum hadn't moved, and neither had Grandpa Pete. The nurse smiled when she saw the big bunch of sunflowers Tara was holding, tied with green twine.
"We don't normally allow flowers," she whispered. "But just this once. They'll be the first thing he sees when he wakes up."

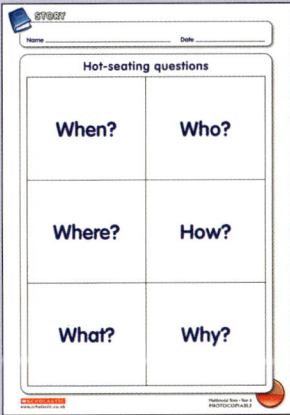

Hot-seating questions

When?	Who?
Where?	How?
What?	Why?

Illustrations © Andrew Stephens/ Beehive Illustration

Vandals!

Objectives

- Strand 4: Improvise using a range of drama strategies and conventions to explore themes such as hopes, fears and desires.
- Strand 7: Understand underlying themes, causes and points of view.

Differentiation

Support
- Use speaking and listening activities to support the development of individual or group playscripts.

Extend
- The children can record (either video or audio) their own playscripts.

Cross-curricular activities

PSHE
- Discuss how the children can deal with a situation in which someone is trying to persuade them to do something that they don't really want to do.

How the text works

- Ask the children, in pairs, to discuss what they know about playscripts. Take feedback and explore their experience of playscripts; have they read them, performed them, seen plays, heard plays?

- Focus on the children's experience of written playscripts and explore their knowledge and understanding of the features of this text type (for example, layout, inclusion of stage directions, and use of adverbs to aid delivery of dialogue).

Screen 1

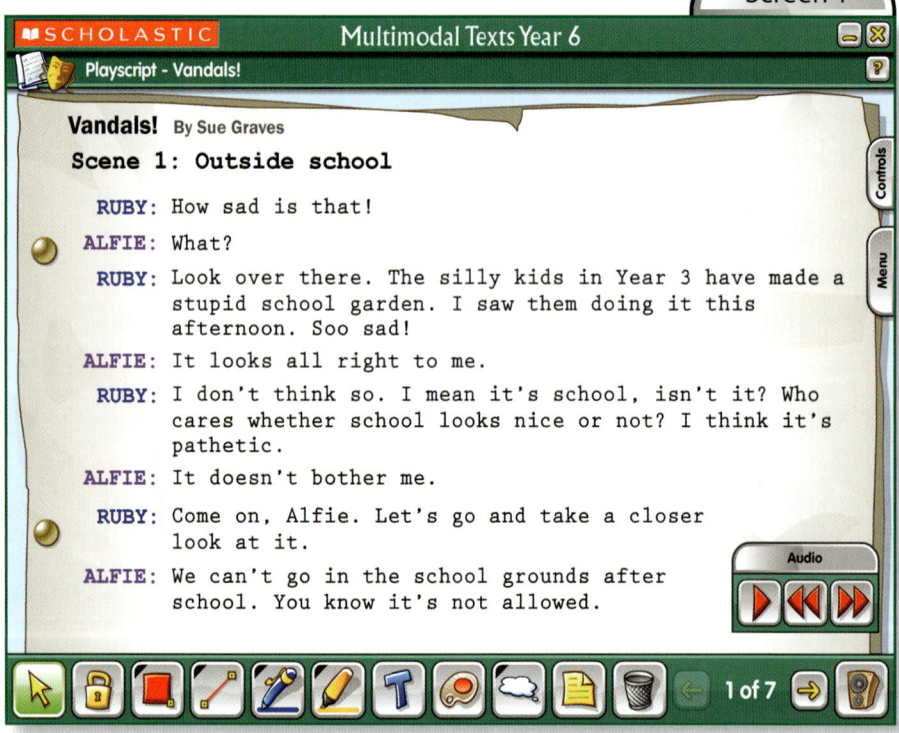

- Discuss the purpose and audience of written playscripts, again linking this to the children's knowledge of structural and linguistic features.

- Explain that they are going to listen to a play being performed and that they will hear it a number of times, each time with a different listening focus.

- Give the children the opportunity to listen to the play, asking them to think about the content of the storyline, specifically about the lesson or moral of the play. Allow a few minutes for paired discussion and then take feedback. Ask: *What lesson can be learned from this play?* (We should respect other people's work and property.)

Screen 2

- Listen to the play again, or read it. This time, ask the children to focus and make notes on the main events. Take feedback and develop a class storyboard (either in words or pictures) that outlines the main events. Discuss the possible timescale over which the play takes place.

- Ask the children to identify the number of characters in the play. (Three.) Ask them to listen to the play again, this time using photocopiable page 42 'Responding to

SCHOLASTIC
www.scholastic.co.uk

characters' to note down their perceptions of the personalities of the three characters. Take feedback, encouraging the children to refer back to the play to support their observations. Discuss which character(s) they can relate to, who they like and/or dislike and why.

Responding to the text

● Explore the children's views as to which of the characters is stronger than the others and how she (Ruby) exerts her influence. As a class, consider how Alfie might have resisted Ruby's persuasive techniques. Develop this through paired role-play activities.

● Explore the evidence the reader can use to make judgements about the characters (for example, what the character said, how they said it and what they did).

● Split the class into three groups. As they listen to the play again, group 1 should focus on character 1 (Ruby), group 2 on character 2 (Alfie) and group 3 on character 3 (Dominic). Ask the groups to think about and note down what the actors needed to know in order to read their lines effectively. As the children feed back their responses, establish the concept that stage directions inform the actors' delivery of lines.

● Play the recording again. This time ask the class to focus purely on the sound effects that are used. Ask: *What is the purpose of the sound effects and what do they add?* (Reality and atmosphere.) In small groups, ask the children to explore how the sound effects could be created in a recording situation.

● In groups of three, ask the children to re-enact the play. Encourage them to think about the extra information that would need to be given in the playscript to support actors in their delivery of the dialogue.

Writing activities

● To prepare the children for writing, support them in thinking about other situations where one person might try to persuade another to do something against their better judgement. Develop these scenarios through role play, hot-seating and other drama activities.

● Through shared and guided writing activities, create and develop playscripts based on the drama activities. Focus on the use of stage directions to give information to actors about delivery of dialogue. Develop an awareness of the purpose and use of sound effects.

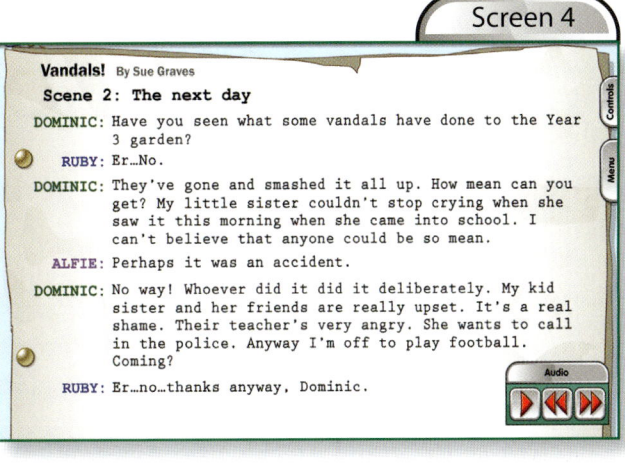

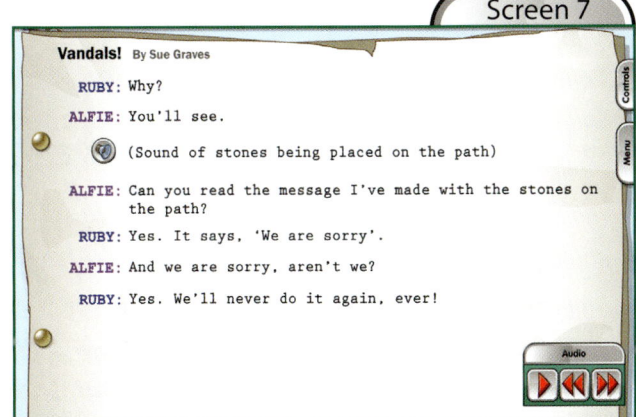

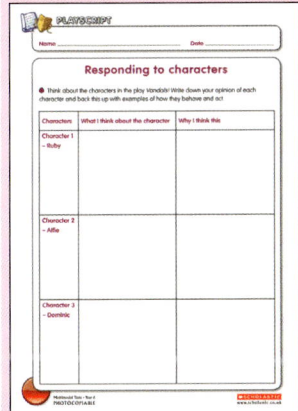

Assessment

● As the class listens to the play, ask the children to evaluate it in terms of content (for example, storyline and quality of performance).

Reference to *100 Literacy Framework Lessons*

● Narrative Unit 3 Authors and texts pages 41–54

Photocopiable

● See page 42 or CD-ROM.

Salmon Says

Objectives

● Strand 2: Analyse and evaluate how speakers present points effectively through use of language and gesture.
● Strand 7: Understand underlying themes, causes and points of view.

Differentiation

Support
● The children can develop bullet pointed lists under the headings 'For' and 'Against'.
Extend
● Support the children in weaving together effective arguments and counter arguments, rather than keeping them as separate paragraphs.

Cross-curricular activities

Science Unit 4B Habitats
● Ask the children to list any questions they have about salmon and their journeys from the sea to their spawning grounds. They can research these questions using available books, magazines and the internet. The children can then produce salmon fact files based on their findings.

How the text works

● Ask the children to discuss, in pairs, what they think a good poetry reading should sound like (for example, reading with expression, varying pace and speaking clearly). Discuss the children's responses and agree on two or three criteria that they should listen out for.

● Play the poem without showing the images. Ask: *How well did the poem meet the agreed criteria? What do you think the poem was about?* If necessary, replay the poem to allow the children to concentrate on the subject matter. Tell the children that the title of the poem is *Salmon Says*. Ask: *Do you know what a salmon is? What do you know about the fish? Who do you think is speaking in the poem?* (A salmon.) *Who are they speaking to?* (Humans.)

● Explain that you are going to play the poem again. Encourage the children to listen carefully, focusing on the pictures that are created in their heads. Explore their responses, asking them to explain and elaborate on the particular words and phrases that enhanced their visualisation.

● Play the poem again, this time showing the images. Are the images on the screen anything like the ones they visualised? Ask: *Do the images change your understanding or enjoyment of the poem?*

● Focus on the sound effects. Ask: *Do they enhance the impact and meaning of the poem?*

SCHOLASTIC
www.scholastic.co.uk

Screen 2

SALMON SAYS
by Celia Warren

And now we are proud of our offspring.
They will dance their parents' dance.
They, too, will follow the scent back home,
We salmon leave nothing to chance.
Poor you, with your cars and ships and planes;
Your rockets that fly to the moon!
You can't even smell or taste your way
To yesterday afternoon!

Illustrations © Mike Lacey/Beehive Illustration

Responding to the text

- Ask the children to reflect on their responses to the poem. Share some of the responses as a class, encouraging the children to refer to the poem. Ask: *Is there anything you like or dislike about it? Are you left puzzled or uncertain about anything? Do you notice any patterns?* (For example, rhyme, rhythm or repetition.)

- Refer to the mention of a *dance* in the poem. Ask: *Why do you think that the poet uses this image?* Discuss the movement of the salmon.

- Focus on the rhyming pattern of the poem and identify which words rhyme. Draw the children's attention to the use of internal rhymes (for example, *savoured* and *waves*; *traced* and *taste*). Ask the children to identify other examples and explore how these add to the flow and impact of the poem.

- Show the children the first line of the poem and establish what the five senses are (sight, sound, touch, taste, smell). Work through the rest of the poem, asking them to identify which of the senses are referred to (taste, smell). Hand out copies of photocopiable page 43 'Looking at the senses' for them to complete; they revisit the poem and find words that are specific to these two senses (for example, *savoured, flavour, taste, scent, smell*). Explore what the poem tells the reader about the behaviour of salmon. Ask: *What does the poem tell us that salmon can do, compared with humans?*

- If the children are unfamiliar with the format of a formal debate explain how they operate (see page 12, *Building on a flood plain*).

- Encourage them to take part in a whole-class debate around the proposal 'This house believes that salmon are cleverer than human beings'. If the children are inexperienced debaters, you may wish to take on the role of chair person yourself.

Writing activities

- Explain to the children that they are going to write up the content of the debate as a discussion text. Revise the typical structural features of discussion texts and the typical language features (for example, using logical connectives). Support the children, through shared and guided writing, in developing and completing their work.

Illustrations © Mike Lacey/Beehive Illustration

Whiteboard tools

- Whiteboard tools used on the screen shots include:
  - Line tool
  - Text tool
  - Colours used ● ●

Assessment

- Review the children's participation in the class debate. Were they all able to make a contribution? Did they take turns and listen to the views of others? Were they able to articulate their views? Could they use Standard English appropriately?

Reference to *100 Literacy Framework Lessons*

- Non-fiction Unit 3 Argument pages 103–118

Photocopiable

- See page 43 or CD-ROM.

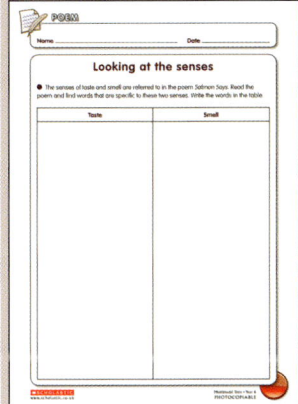

SCHOLASTIC
www.scholastic.co.uk

Objectives

- Strand 2: Make notes when listening for a sustained period and discuss how note-taking varies depending on context and purpose.
- Strand 7: Understand how writers use different structures to create coherence and impact.

Differentiation

Support
- Support the children in reading the transcript, reflecting on how they could improve the reading (for example, through emphasis or by changing the pace and tone of voice). Encourage them to annotate the transcript in the light of this.

Extend
- The children can record their podcasts and, where possible, broadcast them to their identified audience. They can then discuss the audience's reaction and responses with them. Explore any changes they would make to their podcasts in the light of this discussion.

Cross-curricular activities

ICT Unit 6A
Multimedia presentation
- The children can record podcasts about a particular event that they have studied as part of the history curriculum.

News from the allotment

How the text works

- Ask the children, in pairs, to discuss what they know about podcasts. Take feedback and develop a class definition of a podcast.

- Explain that they are going to listen carefully to a podcast. Ask: *Who is broadcasting?* (Amy Williams, a Year 6 pupil.) *What is the podcast about?* (News from a school allotment.) *What is its purpose and audience?* (To inform; the other children and parents.) *Where could it be heard?* (School e-newsletter.) You may wish to give the children photocopiable page 44 'News from the allotment' to support them in this activity. Discuss the children's responses.

- Play the podcast again, asking the children to focus on and identify the organisation of the content (for example, hello, good news, bad news, future plans, goodbye). Discuss the effectiveness of the organisation. Ask: *Would you change it in any way?*

News from the allotment

Hello, this is Amy Williams with the summer term report from the Year 6 allotment. First I'm going to give you some good news. This morning saw the first harvest of tomatoes. We planted these back in June when they were seedlings about 15cm tall. But these aren't ordinary tomatoes, they are purple and they are absolutely delicious! After we picked them we were each able to have a taste and I'm now a big tomato fan.

We have also been growing mange tout. This is a French word that means 'eat all' and that is just what you do. They look rather like flat beans and you can eat the pod and the peas inside. They can be eaten raw or cooked. We are picking

- Split the class into three groups. Allocate each group a section: 'good news'; 'bad news'; 'future plans'. Each group must listen carefully to their section of the podcast and note down the key facts and information given. (You could display, or provide the children with copies of the transcript, for this activity.) Discuss the note-taking strategies the children are aware of (for example, identifying important information, disregarding irrelevant information, listening for key words, using abbreviations and grouping facts on a mind map).

- Play the podcast and ask the groups to take notes. Each group feeds back their findings to the class who consider the quality and relevance of the notes, offering constructive comments as to how they could be improved.

- Remind the children of the audience that they identified for the podcast. Ask: *Do you feel the organisation, style and language used is appropriate for the audience?* Encourage them to offer appropriate and/ or inappropriate examples.

SCHOLASTIC
www.scholastic.co.uk

Responding to the text

- Remind the children of the purpose of this podcast (to inform). Introduce the idea that podcasts should also be entertaining, to keep the audience listening. Ask the children, in groups, to consider how the presenter can attract and keep an audience's attention. Take feedback and list each group's responses.

- Replay the podcast, asking the class to consider whether the presenter has managed to keep their attention and whether the points on the previously recorded list have been covered. Ask: *Would you like to add any more points to the list, having heard the podcast again?*

- Ask the children to consider whether they would have preferred the information given in the podcast to be presented in a paper-based format. Explore their responses and the reasons for them. Ask the children, in groups, to use the notes they made on the podcast previously to talk about and sketch out a rough outline of how such a paper-based text could look (for example, a leaflet, poster or newsletter).

- Encourage the groups to think of alternative ways of presenting the information about the school allotment (for example, video, audio or digital images).

Writing activities

- Explain to the children that they are going to write their own podcast. Use an appropriate newspaper article about a local event or a recent school event as the stimulus. Support the children in identifying the main features of the event (when and where it happened, who was involved, what happened). As a class, decide on an audience for the podcast (parents, other classes). Ask the children to plan and write a script for their podcast. Once the script is complete, encourage them to consider how they would read the script, bearing in mind the need to both inform and entertain their audience.

News from the allotment

protect them from these greedy birds.

Moving onto our future plans. We spent an hour in the allotment last week talking to the Year 5 class, explaining what we've been doing. We all voted on which vegetables to plant for next year because Year 6 won't be at this school then and Year 5 will be looking after the allotment. We decided that quick growing crops would be best so that there will be something to pick in the autumn term. So, beetroot, French beans and winter salad leaves will be planted in the next few weeks.

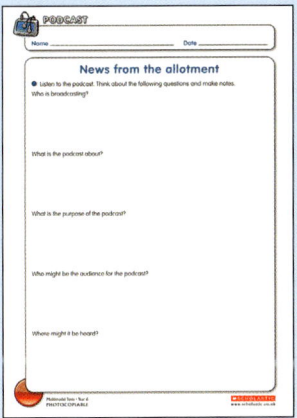

Now Playing
News from the allotment

PODCAST

News from the allotment transcript

Hello, this is Amy Williams with the summer term report from the Year 6 allotment. First I'm going to give you some good news. This morning saw the first harvest of tomatoes. We planted these back in June when they were seedlings about 15cm tall. But these aren't ordinary tomatoes, they are purple and they are absolutely delicious! After we picked them we were each able to have a taste and I'm now a big tomato fan.

We have also been growing mange tout. This is a French word that means 'eat all' and that is just what you do. They look rather like flat beans and you can eat the pod and the peas inside. They can be eaten raw or cooked. We are picking mange tout almost every day at the moment.

Another success in the allotment has been spinach which, as we all know, is Popeye's favourite food. Spinach is very good for you because it contains lots of vitamins, iron and calcium. But, it is not popular with everyone in Year 6 as some children found that the taste was too strong for them.

And now for the bad news, our crop of lettuces has been completely wiped out. Not by disease, slugs or insects but by birds, sparrows to be precise. At first we weren't sure what was eating the plants but Mr Rhodes, our school caretaker, told us that he saw a whole flock of sparrows feasting on our juicy lettuce plants. He is going to make a wooden frame and cover it with netting that will go over the row of lettuces to protect them from these greedy birds.

Moving onto our future plans. We spent an hour in the allotment last week talking to the Year 5 class, explaining what we've been doing. We all voted on which vegetables to plant for next year because Year 6 won't be at this school then and Year 5 will be looking after the allotment. We decided that quick growing crops would be best so that there will be something to pick in the autumn term. So, beetroot, French beans and winter salad leaves will be planted in the next few weeks.

We'd like to wish Year 5 best of luck with the allotment and hope that they enjoy it as much as we have.
Goodbye from Amy Williams at the Year 6 allotment.

Multimodal Texts • Year 6
PHOTOCOPIABLE
SCHOLASTIC
www.scholastic.co.uk

Assessment

- Ask the children to consider the structure and organisation of each other's podcasts. Were they presented in a coherent order? Were facts about similar aspects grouped together? Would they suggest any changes?

Reference to *100 Literacy Framework Lessons*

- Non-fiction Unit 2 Journalistic writing pages 87–102

Photocopiable

- See page 44 or CD-ROM.

PODCAST

Name _____ Date _____

News from the allotment

● Listen to the podcast. Think about the following questions and make notes.
Who is broadcasting?

What is the podcast about?

What is the purpose of the podcast?

Who might be the audience for the podcast?

Where might it be heard?

Multimodal Texts • Year 6
PHOTOCOPIABLE

News from the allotment

plant for next year because Year 6 won't be at this school then and Year 5 will be looking after the allotment. We decided that quick growing crops would be best so that there will be something to pick in the autumn term. So, beetroot, French beans and winter salad leaves will be planted in the next few weeks.

We'd like to wish Year 5 best of luck with the allotment and hope that they enjoy it as much as we have.
Goodbye from Amy Williams at the Year 6 allotment.

x

WaterAid advert

Objectives

● Strand 7: Appraise a text quickly, deciding on its value, quality or usefulness.
● Strand 7: Understand how writers use different structures to create coherence and impact.

Differentiation

Support

● Work with the children as they identify the persuasive techniques that the advert uses, reminding them of other persuasive texts they have read. Discuss why the techniques are persuasive. Do they understand that adverts might be persuading them to do or buy something that they might not necessarily want?

Extend

● The children can compare a selection of paper-based adverts, annotating them as they identify the persuasive techniques used. They can choose the adverts they feel are most successful, and write a brief paragraph that explains why.

Cross-curricular activities

PE Unit 1
Dance activities (1)

● In groups, the children practise walking and running in unison to the rhythm of this and other chants.

How the text works

● Tell the children that they are going to hear a recording that was made for radio. As they listen to it for the first time, ask them to note down anything they notice about the recording.

● Take feedback from the children and develop a class list of observations.

● Play the recording again and ask: *What is the purpose of the recording? What is it trying to achieve?* Take feedback and establish that it is a persuasive text in the form of a radio advert.

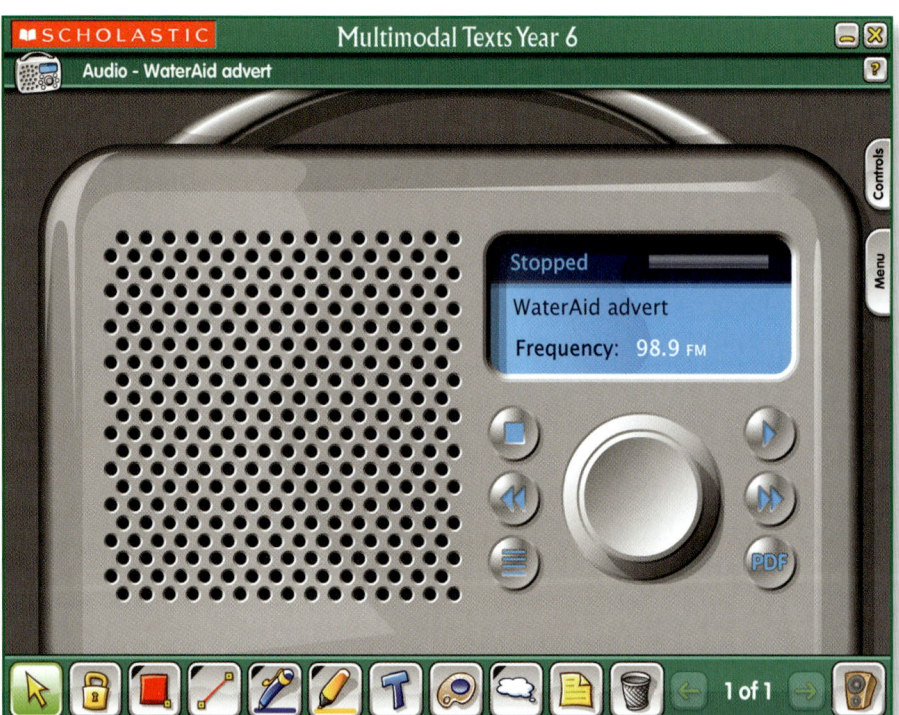

● Discuss what it is trying to persuade listeners to do (take part in a sponsored walk). Ask: *Which organisation is arranging the walk?* (WaterAid.) *What are they planning to do with the money raised?* (Help people who don't have access to clean water.) Explore the children's knowledge and experience of sponsored events.

WaterAid advert	
Voice 1	I don't know but I've been told
Voices 2 and 3	I don't know but I've been told
Voice 1	Walking's good for young and old.
Voices 2 and 3	Walking's good for young and old.
Voice 1	I don't know but I have heard
Voices 2 and 3	I don't know but I have heard

Responding to the text

● Play the advert again and ask the children to respond using photocopiable page 45 'Charity radio advert'. They should discuss their responses with a partner. Take feedback, asking the children to support their responses with reasons. Use this activity to reinforce the idea that one person's likes can be another's dislikes.

● Explain that they are

going to hear the advert again, and should focus on the persuasive techniques being used. After they have heard the advert they should discuss the techniques that they have identified with a partner (for example, repetition, catchy rhymes). Take feedback from the paired discussions.

● Revisit the list of observations made earlier. Were any of them related to the persuasive techniques they have identified?

● Ask the children why they think the advert is presented in the form of a rhyming chant. (It's catchy and memorable.) Why do they think this is important in terms of a radio advert? (It makes the listener want to join in with the chant and, therefore, get involved in the fund-raising effort.)

● Explore the use of rhythm in the advert. Ask: *What impact does it have on you, as a listener? Why do you think the advert uses this rhythm?* Explain that the advert is based on chants that armed forces use when marching. Discuss why troops might use the chant (for example, to march in unison or to maintain a regular speed).

● Replay the advert, concentrating on the spoken section at the end. Ask: *What information is being given?* (Background to the appeal and to WaterAid's work. What action to take next.) *Why do you think this information wasn't included in the chant?* (It's important and needs to be heard clearly. It might have been too difficult to fit into the rhyme and rhythm of the chant.)

● Ask the children to vote on the success of the advert in achieving its aim.

Writing activities

● In small groups, ask the children to write their own chants using the advert as a model. Once written, they can practise chanting in unison and then record their chants. They may wish to add other sound effects. The children can produce a paper-based advert using the information from the radio advert.

Assessment

● Check the children's knowledge and understanding of the typical structural and linguistic features of persuasive texts.

Reference to *100 Literacy Framework Lessons*

● Revision Unit 2 Non-fiction page 175

Photocopiable

● See page 45 or CD-ROM.

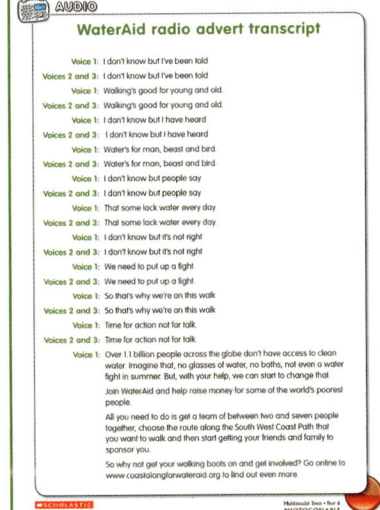

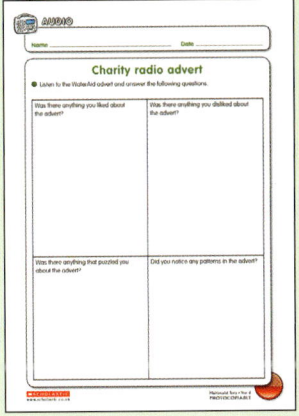

www.scholastic.co.uk

Dr Barnardo

Objectives

● Strand 4: Improvise using a range of drama strategies and conventions to explore themes such as hopes, fears and desires.
● Strand 7: Understand underlying themes, causes and points of view.

Differentiation

Support
● Help the children to make connections between what they see in images and their own knowledge and experience. Demonstrate how your own thinking makes links between what is seen and what is known.

Extend
● Encourage the children to support observations about images with evidence based on what they can see and what they know.

Cross-curricular activities

History Unit 18
What was it like to live here in the past?
● The children can research the life and times of Dr Barnardo.

PSHE
● The children can research the current work of the Barnardo's charity.

How the text works and responding to the text

● Explain to the children that they are going to concentrate on reading a series of images. Discuss how they think they can 'read' pictures. Make explicit that a reader can describe what they see in a picture, and can also make links between this and their own knowledge and experiences, in order to make deductions and inferences.

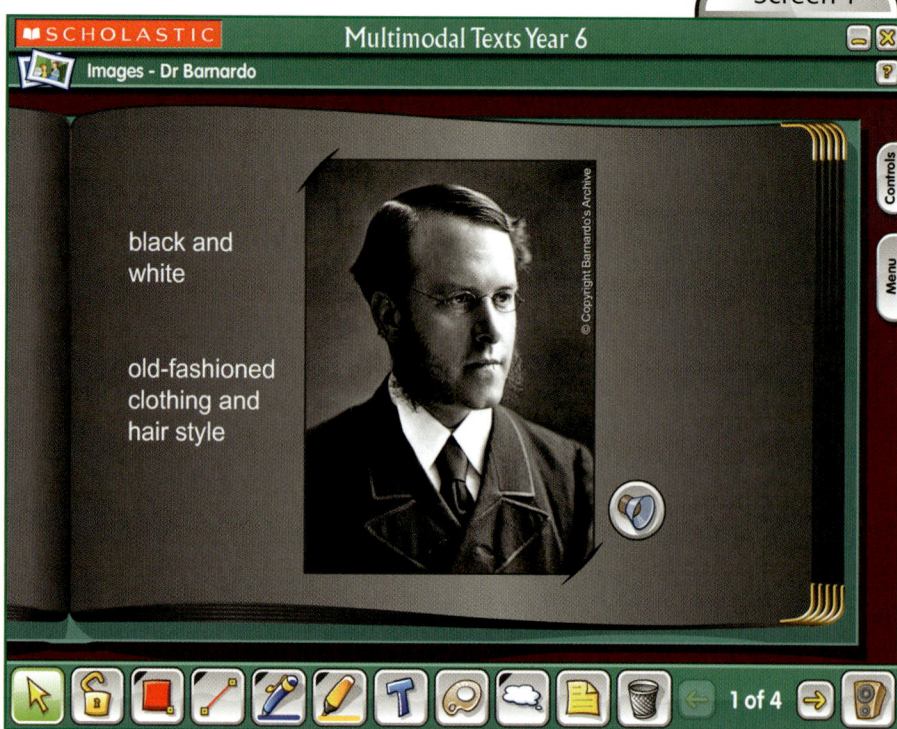

● Show the children the image of Dr Barnardo. Ask them to describe what they can see in the picture (a man). Ask: *When do you think the photograph was taken? What clues are there in the photograph that tell us that it was taken long ago?* (Clothing, hairstyle, black and white photograph.) Listen to the music, what does this add to the image? Invite pairs to discuss their impression of the man in the photograph.

● Tell the children that the photo is of Thomas Barnardo, one of the most famous men in Victorian Britain. He was born in Dublin and came to London in 1866 to train as a doctor. When he arrived in London, he found thousands of children sleeping on the streets, and many others begging. He was so concerned about the situation of London's children that he set up a school for them.

● Show the children the next picture. Ask: *What differences do you notice between this image and the last one?* (This one is a drawing, the last was a photograph). *Why do you think this picture was drawn, rather than photographed?*

SCHOLASTIC
www.scholastic.co.uk

- Ask the children to think about what their eye is drawn to when they first look at the drawing (the figures in the foreground). Ask: *Who do you think these figures are?* (Dr Barnardo and Jim Jarvis, a boy from Barnardo's school.) *What details can you see in the background of the drawing? Can you suggest what Jim Jarvis is showing Dr Barnardo?* (Homeless children.)

- Ask the children to role play this scene between Jim and Dr Barnardo. What are they saying to each other?

Screen 3

- Show the children the third image and listen to the sound effect (Barnardo's school in Victorian times). Ask: *When do you think this was taken? What evidence is there?* Encourage the children to look at the details of the clothing and the buildings in the image. *How do you think the children in the photograph were feeling? How would you feel if you were at the school?*

- Explain that Dr Barnardo went on to set up many schools for orphaned children and that his work continues today, as a charity. However, the focus now is different; the charity concentrates on helping children who are disadvantaged, rather than children who have lost their parents.

- Show the children the fourth image. Ask for their response to the image. Using photocopiable page 46 'Reading the picture', ask the children to record their responses. They could use one colour for recording how they feel about one of the people and a different colour to record what they think the person is like.

- Ask the children to reflect on the four images and explore how we often make judgements about people purely based on appearance.

Writing activities

- Ask the children to tell you what they know about biographies. Can they distinguish between biography and autobiography? Have any of them read biographies or autobiographies? Explain that they are going to write a short biography of Dr Barnardo. Explore what the children know about him so far, and list these facts. Discuss what else they would like to find out about him, and give them the opportunity to research more of his life. They then plan and write their biography of Dr Barnardo.

Screen 4

Images © Copyright Barnardo's Archive

Whiteboard tools

- Whiteboard tools used on the screen shots include:
  T Text tool
  Colours used

Assessment

- Ask the children questions about images that involve them making literal, inferential and deductive responses. Are they able to support their responses by referring to the image?

Reference to *100 Literacy Framework Lessons*

- Non-fiction Unit 1 Biography and autobiography pages 69–86

Photocopiable

- See page 46 or CD-ROM.

Mount Everest

How the text works and responding to the text

Objectives

● Strand 7: Understand underlying themes, causes and points of view.
● Strand 8: Sustain engagement with [longer] texts, using different techniques to make the text come alive.

Differentiation

Support

● Work with the children as they identify what they can see on the photographs and demonstrate how they can make inferences from the images by linking information with their own knowledge and experiences. The children can use photocopiable page 47 'Responding to photographs' to support and structure their responses.

Extend

● Ask the children to turn their oral responses to the pictures into written responses, supporting their opinions with references to particular aspects of the pictures and their own knowledge.

Cross-curricular activities

Geography Unit 5
The mountain environment
● The children can use the internet to carry out further research into the impact of tourism and global warming on Mount Everest.

● Show the children the first image of Mount Everest from a distance and ask them to tell you what they can see in the picture (a mountain). Explain that this is a literal response; it is just what can be seen.

● Now ask them to make an inference about the image by thinking about what the snow on the mountain tells them. Responses could include 'It is winter' or 'It is high up', depending on the children's knowledge. Draw attention to the fact that there is no snow in the foreground. Ask: *Why do you think there is only snow on the upper part of the mountain?* (It is colder as it is higher up.)

Screen 1

● Show the children the picture on screen 2. Again, ask them to tell you what they can see (climbers or walkers on a snowy landscape). Ask them to discuss the picture with a partner and to make an inference about the image. Focus on the climbers and talk about their clothing and what they are carrying and holding. Ask: *What does this tell us?* (It is cold, walking might be difficult, and they need supplies of some kind.) *Can you make any other inferences from the photograph?* (There is evidence that the snow has melted and refrozen in places, indicating changes in temperature.)

● Explain to the children that these are pictures of Mount Everest. Use a globe or atlas to identify where

Screen 2

■SCHOLASTIC
www.scholastic.co.uk

Mount Everest is. Ask: *Do you know anything about Mount Everest that might help you to read the pictures?*

● Show the children the picture of rubbish against the fence and ask for their response to the image. Explain that this picture was also taken on Mount Everest. Ask: *What do you think the rubbish is? Where did it come from? Why do you think that people throw things away when they are climbing Mount Everest?* (To get rid of unwanted weight.) Tell the children that because Mount Everest is so high it is difficult to breathe, so climbers don't want to carry anything that they no longer need. Ask the children why they think the rubbish has gathered in this particular place. (There is evidence that it is windy, the plastic is blowing to the right, so the rubbish has been blown against the fence.)

● Explain that the amount of rubbish left on Mount Everest is an increasing problem as more and more tourists visit the area and that there have been calls for the mountain to be closed to climbers.

● Show the children the photograph of the campsite. Ask: *Who do you think might have taken this? Where were they standing when it was taken? What evidence can you see that it is windy?* (The clothes to the left of the tent are being blown to the right.)

● Focus on the climbers by the tent. Ask: *What do you think the climbers are doing? How could it feel to be there?* Encourage them to use evidence from the photograph and their knowledge of Mount Everest to support their responses (for example, the climbers are wearing hats and warm clothing, so it must be cold). Ask the children to consider why these climbers, and others, are camping on Mount Everest when it looks so inhospitable.

Writing activities

● Ask the children to work in small groups to discuss and note down the main points about the litter problem on Mount Everest, and to explore ways of solving it. Feed back ideas to the whole class, and encourage the children to offer constructive comments about each others' solutions, suggesting improvements. Explain that they are going to design and produce a poster that gives information about Mount Everest's litter problem, and proposes ways of solving it. Discuss how to make a poster eye-catching and effective (for example, the use of colour, different typefaces, images). Ask each group to turn their earlier ideas into a poster.

Whiteboard tools

● Whiteboard tools used on the screen shots include:
🔍 Outline circle
✎ Line tool
T Text tool
🔴 Colour used

Assessment

● Through observation of paired and group discussion, check the children's ability to make inferences and deductions from the photographs, and to support their opinions by references to the images.

Reference to *100 Literacy Framework Lessons*

● Non-fiction Unit 2 Journalistic writing pages 87–102

Photocopiable

● See page 47 or CD-ROM.

WWW

Name _____

Date _____

Venn diagram

● Think about the features of books and websites and write them in the correct circle in the Venn diagram. If a feature is common to both websites and books, write it where the circles overlap.

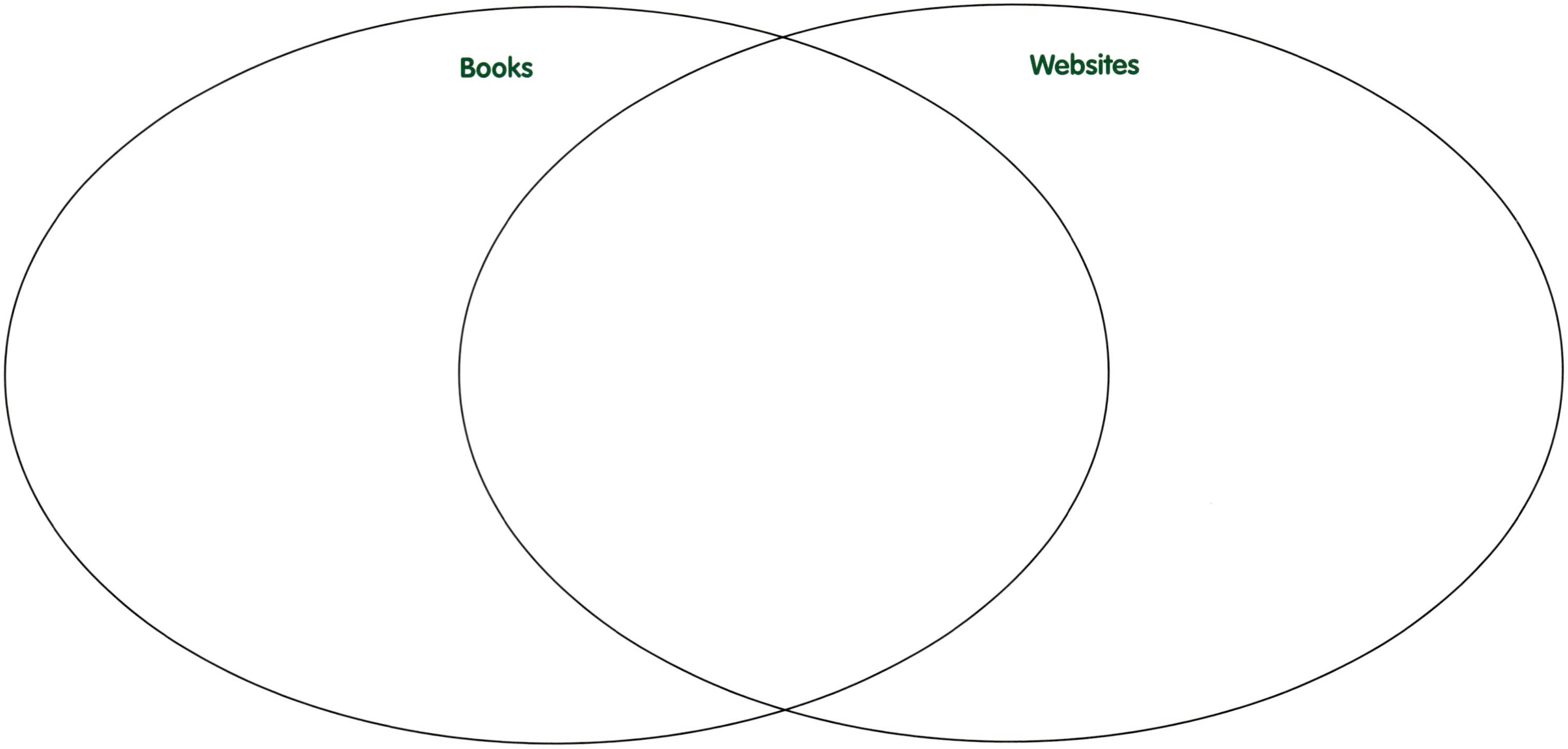

Websites

Books

Multimodal Texts • Year 6

PHOTOCOPIABLE

SCHOLASTIC
www.scholastic.co.uk

Name _____   **Date** _____

Understanding the text

● Look at the *Victorian transport* website. Discuss these questions and write answers.

Why do you think the author has written the word *still* in italics?

What did horses transport in the 1890s?

What do you think the word gentlefolk means?

Can you think of another word for automobile?

What do you think a farrier is?

Name _____ **Date** _____

For and against

● Is it right to make hill walkers keep to a paved path? Think about the arguments for and against the issue on the website and make notes in this table.

For	Against

Multimodal Texts • Year 6
PHOTOCOPIABLE

■SCHOLASTIC
www.scholastic.co.uk

Name _____ **Date** _____

Planning a discussion text

● Plan a discussion text about whether houses should be built on flood plains. Use this page to structure your notes.

The issue:

Arguments for:

Arguments against:

Summing up:

Name _____   **Date** _____

Descriptive thinking

● Imagine you are standing on a cliff top. Think about words and phrases you could use to describe what you can hear, smell, taste and feel. Make a note of these words and phrases and use them when planning your own poem.

Hear	Smell

Taste	Feel

Multimodal Texts • Year 6
PHOTOCOPIABLE
■ SCHOLASTIC
www.scholastic.co.uk

Name _____ **Date** _____

Planning a story

● Use this frame to help you plan your own problem-solving story.

1 Opening: Introduce the characters and setting.
2 Build-up: Describe what the characters did and where they were as the story starts.
3 Complication: Describe the problem that the characters were faced with.
4 Solution: Describe how the characters solved the problem.
5 Ending: Describe where the characters were at the end of the story and how they felt about events.

Name _____   **Date** _____

Role play

● Role play the scene when Ivy and the other evacuees arrive at Christchurch station.

● Think about these questions:

What would it be like to arrive in a strange place without your parents?

How would it feel if other children were chosen before you?

How did Ivy feel about living on a farm?

After your role play, discuss these points and make some notes about what you thought, said and did. Use these notes to help you to write a playscript for the scene.

■SCHOLASTIC
www.scholastic.co.uk

STORY

Hot-seating questions

When?	**Who?**
Where?	**How?**
What?	**Why?**

Name _____   **Date** _____

Responding to characters

● Think about the characters in the play *Vandals!* Write down your opinion of each character and back this up with examples of how they behave and act.

Characters	What I think about the character	Why I think this
Character 1 – Ruby		
Character 2 – Alfie		
Character 3 – Dominic		

Multimodal Texts • Year 6
PHOTOCOPIABLE
SCHOLASTIC
www.scholastic.co.uk

POEM

Name _____   **Date** _____

Looking at the senses

● The senses of taste and smell are referred to in the poem *Salmon Says*. Read the poem and find words that are specific to these two senses. Write the words in the table.

Taste	Smell

S C H O L A S T I C
www.scholastic.co.uk

Name _____   **Date** _____

News from the allotment

● Listen to the podcast. Think about the following questions and make notes.

Who is broadcasting?

What is the podcast about?

What is the purpose of the podcast?

Who might be the audience for the podcast?

Where might it be heard?

■SCHOLASTIC
www.scholastic.co.uk

Name _____   **Date** _____

Charity radio advert

● Listen to the WaterAid advert and answer the following questions.

Was there anything you liked about the advert?	Was there anything you disliked about the advert?
Was there anything that puzzled you about the advert?	**Did you notice any patterns in the advert?**

■ S C H O L A S T I C
www.scholastic.co.uk

Name _____ Date _____

Reading the picture

● Use this page to help you to read the picture.

● Look carefully at the photograph and write what you can see, what you can work out from the photograph and why you have come to your conclusions.

What I know.
What I can work out.
Why I think this.

SCHOLASTIC
www.scholastic.co.uk

Name _____   Date _____

Responding to photographs

Look closely at the images of Everest; they contain a lot of information. Think about the following questions:

● What does each picture tell you?

● What does the detail tell you? What are the people wearing? What is the weather like?

● What do you already know about Everest?

Make notes of your thoughts and observations.

What I can see in the photograph	What this makes me think	Why I think this

SCHOLASTIC
www.scholastic.co.uk

SCHOLASTIC

Also available in this series:

ISBN 978-0439-94577-6

ISBN 978-1407-10013-5

ISBN 978-1407-10014-2

ISBN 978-1407-10015-9

ISBN 978-1407-10016-6

ISBN 978-1407-10017-3

To find out more, call: 0845 603 9091
or visit our website www.scholastic.co.uk